Ancient Egypt

Discovering Ancient Egypt and Egyptian Mythology including History, Pharaohs, Sphinx, Pyramids and More!

Table of Contents

Introduction

I want to thank you and congratulate you for downloading the book, "Ancient Egypt".

This book contains helpful information about Ancient Egypt and Egyptian mythology!

You will soon learn about the many different Egyptian Gods, and the famous stories of their lives. You will also learn about the various creation stories that different groups of Ancient Egyptians believed in.

This book will explain to you the key facets of Egyptian mythology, and will take you through some of the most famous and interesting Ancient Egyptian stories.

You will learn about Gods, worship, Pharaohs, pyramids, and more!

Egyptian mythology is exciting and packed with interesting tales. Read on to discover more!

Thanks again for downloading this book, I hope you enjoy it!

Chapter 1: Major Gods of Egypt

Although it makes sense to start off this book by talking about the creation myths of Egypt, these stories often involve the names of gods associated with controlling the different aspects of daily Egyptian life. Following are the major gods of Egypt and the things/activities they lord over.

Amun

Amun is considered one of the most influential and major gods of Egyptian history. He can be portrayed as a man with a ram head, or a man wearing two plumes of feathers as a headdress. At some point, he was even called the King of the Gods. His power and influence became stronger however, when Amun was combined with the sun god Ra, creating Amun-Ra.

Atum

Dubbed as the god of creation, Atum is often drawn as a man with a long beard. He is believed to be self-created and it will be him who brings the world back to watery chaos during the creation cycle. His cult is mainly found in Heliopolis and in this myth; it is believed that the first tears of Atum resulted in the creation of man. Of course, the same story is said of Ra, the sun god.

Ra

Ra is the sun god and depicted as a man with a hawk's head. He also wears a head dress with a sun disk on top and carries a staff. He was considered one of the most important gods in Egypt since he brought along the sun which meant a new day for the people of Egypt. Egyptians would celebrate every day the sun shines, believing that during the night, Ra traveled through the underworld on his ship and fought gallantly before emerging in the morning. The sun's emergence therefore is a sign that Ra once again won the battle in the River of Duat before providing the much needed light necessary for Egyptian crops to grow. During the night, while traveling through the underworld, Ra's appearance changes with his head turning into the shape of a ram.

A conflicting story of the sun god also notes that instead of traveling through the Duat River, he is instead swallowed by Nut, the goddess of the sky. A major god, there are also Egyptians who believe that Ra is the creator and all other gods followed or were made by him.

Geb

Geb is god of the earth and depicted as a man with trees, hills, and land all over his body. One of the first few gods to emerge according to creation myths, Geb is both husband and brother to the goddess of sky, Nut. According to prophecies, a child of Geb and Nut would one day overthrow Ra from his position as supreme god and for this reason, Geb and Nut were kept apart – which is why the sky is so far away from the earth.

Nut

Her name may also be spelled as Neuth, Newet, and Nuit. The wife of Geb, she is the goddess of the sky and is often drawn as stretching over Geb, her body covered in stars and the blue of the sky. When drawn, she is often shown as having a water jug on her head. She is the mother of Osiris as well as several other gods. True to prophecy, Osiris managed to overthrow Ra and held supreme power over the gods. Of course, in some stories, this wasn't always the case.

Shu (*He Who Rises Up*)

Depictions of Shu almost always show him between Nut and Geb – holding the sky away from the earth as she stretches above him. There's a good reason for this – it was Shu's job to make sure that Nut and Geb would not create a child that could eventually overthrow Ra – of which he was unsuccessful. The god of air, Shu is often seen as a man wearing a headdress with four feathers. He is also the father of Nut and Geb. The meaning of his name is a direct reference to the fact that he 'rises up' between the earth and sky, holding them apart through a large expanse of air –the same element he lords over.

Osiris

Osiris is perhaps one of the most recognized gods in Egyptian mythology. He is the first child of Geb and Nut, and according to stories, he took over the care of the world after the sun god Ra left. However, that's just a small part of the Osiris mythos. Often depicted as a human with blue skin and wearing white robes, Osiris later became known as god of the underworld. He sat in judgment of every person that went to the afterlife. Stories reveal that the Egyptian tradition of mummification originated from Osiris who was also mummified upon his death.

Isis

The wife of Osiris, Isis is portrayed as a loyal and loving wife who contributed largely to the works of her husband and therefore, the peace and prosperity of Egypt during the reign of Osiris. Often portrayed as a woman with a headdress in the shape of a throne, some stories depict Isis as both clever and ambitious, tricking Ra into ascending into the heavens so that Osiris would become King. She can also be drawn as a beautiful woman with her arms spread out and wings protruding from her arms in an array of colors. Mother to Horus, she is the goddess of both magic and nature.

Set *(Setesh, Sutekh, Suty, Sutekh)*

Set is the brother of Osiris and is often shown in a bad light. Not really surprising considering that he's the god of violence, disorder, and desert storms. He is said to be the god of foreigners in the old religion of Egypt. He is often drawn as someone with a red skin and the head of an animal, closely resembling an anteater. He is the father to Anubis and uncle to Horus. In Egyptian mythology, Set was responsible for the death of the well-loved king Osiris through trickery and deceit. After the death of Osiris, Set took over the throne, and according to stories, his reign was not a good one. During the reign of Ra however, it was said that Set took a vital role as he was one of the strongest gods in the line. Set fought the serpent of chaos Apep whenever Ra sailed on his boat, making sure that the sun rose again the next day.

Nephthys *(Nebthet)*

A major goddess, wife of Set and often portrayed as a woman wearing a house and basket headdress, Nephthys is often mistaken to be the goddess of housewives. This is an understandable mistake since her name literally translates to "Lady of the House" but in truth, she is actually a priestess. She is also dubbed the river goddess, and despite being wife to Set, she was kind enough to help Isis gather the body parts of Osiris before Isis restored him to life. Her son with Set, Anubis, is the god of funeral rites.

Horus

Horus, the son of Isis and Osiris, was tasked with the job of avenging his father against his killer, Set. Drawn as a man with the head of a falcon, the battle between Horus and his uncle Set is one of the most significant stories in Egyptian mythology. Horus eventually won the battle, gaining the throne and resuming a better reign over the land. It is believed that every pharaoh that ruled over the land is a descendant of Horus. It is interesting to note that the origins of Horus in mythology aren't always straightforward. Some stories actually say that Horus is the brother of Isis instead of her son. In others, it is believed that Horus is the 'live' manifestation of Osiris. He is also worshipped as the sky god, the god of hunting, and the god of war.

Anubis

Anubis is the son of Set and Nephthys, often portrayed as a man with a jackal for a head. In stories, it was said that he observed in the mummification process, escorting the dead to the hall where they were to be judged. When Osiris died, Anubis was present and helped his mother Nephthys and Isis to bind the dead king together, creating the first mummy. He is also part of the "Weighing of the Heart" process wherein it is determined if the dead can enter the underworld or not. Thanks to his role during the first mummification, priests in ancient Egypt would often wear a mask resembling the head of Anubis during mummification.

Bast

Although a minor god, there's no question that Bast was of great influence in the daily life of Egyptians. Bast is a cat and protected people from bad luck. According to stories, Bast is the cat of the sun god Ra, and people would often wear amulets of her image to ensure protection during the Dead Days. It wasn't just Bast; all cats in Egypt were greatly revered because they took care of the people by killing scorpions, snakes, spiders, and other creatures that may cause harm.

Sobek

Portrayed as a man with a head of a crocodile, Sobek is considered the god of crocodiles. He was both feared and revered, mostly because crocodiles were dangerous in Egypt. Many Egyptians were killed every year by these creatures. According to stories, the Nile River is the result of Sobek's sweat.

Bes

Bes is perhaps the most mysterious Egyptian god. He is portrayed as a dwarf with the mane of a lion, deigned to protect families, children, and mothers. He is supposed to scare off evil spirits and in Egypt, wearing an amulet of Bes is a general sign of good luck. As a dwarf, Egyptians are of the opinion that Bes is inherently magical. In fact, everyone who was born a little different in the land was considered a form of magic.

Ma'at

The daughter of Ra, Ma'at is the goddess associated with truth, harmony and justice. Pharaohs often make offerings to her to show that they hold true to everything the goddess stands for. Ma'at is often pictured with a single feather on her head.

Ogdoad

Ogdoad is not a god but rather, the collective term used when talking about a group of gods. It roughly translates to 'eightfold', referring to the eight gods that were primarily worshiped in Hermopolis. These eight gods include: Nu and Naunet, Amun and Amaunet, Huh and Hauhet, Kuk and Kauket.

Ennead

The Ennead is much like Ogdoad in the sense that it refers to a collection of gods in Egyptian mythology. Unlike Ogdoad, there are nine deities in the Ennead and these nine are mostly worshiped in Heliopolis. These nine gods and goddesses include: Atum, Shu, Tefnut, Geb, Nut, Osiris, Isis, Set, and Nephthys.

Of course, those are just few of the gods in ancient Egypt. Other ones include:

- Tefnut – the goddess of moisture, she is a woman with the head of a lioness

- Khonsu – the god of the moon, he is portrayed as a young man with a crescent on top of his head.

- Babi – god of wild baboons, Babi resided in the underworld and ate the remains of evil people

- Tawaret – the goddess of hippos, she is obviously depicted as a hippopotamus and seen as a general source of good luck. Often drawn as having a pregnant belly, stories said that Tawaret is mostly protective of pregnant women.

- Hathor – a woman with a headdress in the shape of a sun disk with cow ears. Hathor is said to be the wife of Horus and the goddess of joy and love.

- Khnum – depicted as man with a curly-horned ram for a head. It is believed the Khnum is a creator god who used a potter's wheel to mould people from the clay of the Nile.

- Hapy – drawn as a man with a pot belly, Hapy brought floods to the Nile River every year which resulted in a steady flow of water for Egyptian crops.

- Thoth – a man holding a palette for writing, Egyptians believed that it was from Thoth that they learned Hieroglyphics. He is the god of knowledge and writing.

- Seshat – often drawn as a woman wearing a dress made of panther skin, Seshat was the goddess of writing and measurement.

- Sekhmet – the goddess of war, she had the head of a lioness

- Khepri – believed to be the god of creation, rebirth, and the movement of the sun – Khepri is often drawn as a man with a scarab beetle for a head.

Most of the gods are drawn with an ankh in one hand and a scepter in another. The ankh is a symbol of eternal life – which makes sense since it is carried by gods believed to be immortal.

Chapter 2: Creation Stories

Like Roman and Greek myths, Egyptian myths are wide, varied, creative, and highly interesting. When it comes to creation, ancient Egypt accepts several possible theories, but there are specific elements that seem to appear throughout these different ideas.

Essentially, there are four basic creation myths, associated with a particular god favored by the four major cities. All four myths have two things in common: that the world arose from the water *Nu* and that the first thing that came out was *benben,* a mound shaped like a pyramid.

Heliopolis

The self-engendered god in the Heliopolis version is *Atum* who came from the waters of Nu. Originally an inert potential being, there's a sexual element to how *Atum* gave rise to the different gods and goddesses that govern every other creation. In the stories, it is said that *Atum* masturbated using his hand as a representation of the female element. It is believed that there's an inherent female and male quality in *Atum* which makes this possible.

The creation process gave birth to a total of 8 gods, although Atum was only directly responsible for the two of them: Shu and Tefnut which he "sneezed" and "spat" according to legends. It started with *Shu,* the air god followed by *Tefnut,* corresponding to the arrival of empty space in the endless waters. These two gods produced Geb and Nut – the gods of earth and sky respectively

Again, the offspring of Shu and Tefnut coupled and this time, four children were produced: Osiris, Isis, Nephthys, and Set. These four represented the four forces of life with Osiris being the god of fertility, Isis of motherhood, Nephthys of female sexuality and her counterpart, Set, the god of male sexuality.

Hermopolis

In the Hermopolis creation myth, the waters of Nu are also considered a god, paired with a female counterpart called Naunet. Other gods include Amun and Amaunet, the hidden and unknowable nature, Huh and Hauhet representing the infinite extent of the water, and Kuk and Kauket – the darkness found in the water. The creation process itself is vague with the Hermopolis myth stating that these different gods converged, resulting to the creation of benben, the mound. Focusing mainly on how the world was before everything else was created, the myth depicts the different gods and goddesses as creatures of the sea. As if maintaining balance, the myth held to the male-female counterparts with the male gods depicted as frogs and the women as snakes. After the joining of all the gods, the sun and sky also emerged together with the mound.

Memphis

Patron of craftsmen, Ptah is the god believed to be the seat of creation in the Memphite version. Because of his ability to visualize and craft raw products, he is credited with the process of creating the world. Instead of grabbing raw materials however, the creation was of an intellectual nature with ancient Egyptians believing that it originated from Ptah's heart. Now, this might seem contradictory – but it's important to note that Egyptians originally considered the heart as the 'center of thought'. The visions were finally turned into reality when Ptah spoke the words out loud and the world came into being.

Thebes

In the Thebian creation myth, it was believed that Amun was the source of everything. Defined as the source of all things, Thebians believed that all the gods responsible for creation were simply different aspects of Amun. Although there were no specifics on exactly how this occurred, Thebians believed that Amun went beyond the typical boundaries of creation. He was deeper than the underworld and higher than the sky, and even other gods had no idea of his true nature. The fact that many believed Thebes to be the location of where *benben* emerged may also have fueled the popularity of Amun, despite the existence of other creation myths. The major religion capital of Egypt, you'll find various representations of the gods in Egyptian art and architecture. Amun was such a distinguished god that he was hailed as the supreme god lording over the Egyptian pantheon.

You'll notice that the creation myths don't exactly oppose each other but instead, provide different aspects of the same story, as if picking up where the other one left off.

Despite the differences in the creation myths however, Egyptians stayed true to the praise and worship of their gods as can be seen through their everyday life.

Ra the Creator *(Re)*

In some stories, it was believed that Ra was the ultimate creator – and he shows up often enough in Egyptian writings to make this possible. According to stories, Ra wept and it was from these tears that the first man came into being. He cut himself and created Hu (authority) and Sia (mind) and it was him who was responsible for creating the seasons. In the story of Ra as the ultimate creator, Egyptians believed that Ra was self-created or that other gods were simply different manifestations of Ra.

Chapter 3: Stories of Egyptian Gods

The stories of Egyptian gods are varied and in some places, somewhat conflicting. It is interesting to note however that unlike Greek gods, the gods of Egypt aren't exactly seen as 'immortal' – as with the case of Osiris who still died in the hands of Set. The gods are also not inherently 'good' or 'bad' but rather, a mixture of positive and negative personalities in every story. As with the case of Set, although the god of violence is often seen in a bad light, there are stories and legends of Set where he actually turns out as the good guy.

Story of Isis' Trickery

Despite the fact that Isis was portrayed as a good and loving goddess, the origin of exactly how Osiris and Horus – Isis' husband and son – claimed the throne doesn't show the goddess in a very good light. It started with the passing of time and the sun god Ra, in the form of a man, starting to grow old. As with most elders, Ra was having a hard time ruling his land and it did not help that the people he ruled over mocked him for his advancing age.

During one of his walks, spittle fell from his mouth and dropped on the desert. Isis took the resulting mud and created a snake – the first cobra – and laid it on Ra's path for it to bite him when he walked past. The cobra since them became the sign for Egyptian queens as can be seen in many films.

The cobra did bite the aging sun god and when it did, the snake made from clay disappeared, leaving its venom to flow through the veins of Ra. Feeling great pain, Ra cried out, unable to believe that anything he created would dare hurt him in any way. But the pain was great indeed – and Ra – though able to bring life to anything just by speaking its name – was unable to heal himself.

All the gods Ra created came to him, but it was Isis –the goddess of magic who promised to cure him. She urged Ra to tell her his Secret Name, the name which was in his heart – for this was the most powerful name that Isis could use to cure the ailing king.

Ra replied: "I am Builder of the Mountains. I am Source of the Waters throughout all the world. I am Light and Darkness. I am Creator of the Great River of Egypt. I am the Kindler of the Fire that burns in the sky; yes, I am Khepera in the morning, Re at the noontide, and Tum in the evening."

However, this was not the name Isis was looking for – these were all the names that man had given Ra. The goddess urged him once more and finally, Ra allowed the name to pass from his heart to the heart of Isis, giving the magic goddess the Name of Power.

Isis finally uttered his name and healed the king – but he could no longer reign down on earth. Instead, the old god ascended to the heavens where he looked upon everything he created.

According to stories, Ra made Isis promise never to tell anyone of the name, except for her son which will be called Horus and that Horus too must keep the Name of Power a secret – a promise which was kept. It was this knowledge of Horus that played a part in his eventual win against Set and claiming the throne of Egypt as the first pharaoh.

Story of Osiris: From Overlord King to the Underworld

Osiris, the eldest son of Nut and Geb became the ruler of all things after the sun god Ra ascended to the heavens. His birth was signaled by a voice from the heavens saying: Now hath come the lord of all things. During his time as the lord of all Egypt, Osiris was well liked, ushering in a time of prosperity for the country. Before he sat on the throne, ancient Egyptians lived like savages, living off the land mostly through hunting. It was said that Osiris gave them the gift of fire, created laws, issued decrees, and ruled with great wisdom. His wife – Isis – was equally intelligent and helped Osiris teach men about farming, how to plow the land and harvest for a steady supply of food. He also taught them to worship, erecting temples in honor of the gods. Simply put, the reign of Osiris was a good time with Egyptians living in harmony rather than fighting with each other for survival.

After realizing the good he had brought the people of Egpyt, Osiris decided to travel the world and spread peace and goodness through every nook of the land. He was successful in this conquest, his ability to persuade with words of wisdom bringing forth times of rejoicing in every place he visited. While the great king Osiris was gone, Isis took on the role of ruling over Egypt and she was equally wise and kind as her husband.

Now, let's not forget that Osiris also has several siblings, one of which is Set. Set is a lover of warfare and he was envious of all the things Osiris managed to achieve. According to stories, Set only had seventy-two followers, but with his evil cunning, he managed to think of a way to get rid of Osiris upon his return to Egypt.

What Set did was simple: he had a dazzling chest specially made with a shape that perfectly fit the proportions of the King. He brought it to the welcome party of Osiris and every guest looked on the chest with envy and desired it for himself. As if proposing a game, Set revealed that he would give the chest to anyone who would fit exactly within the container. Of course – it was made to the King's exact specifications, which is why when one person after another tried to fit inside, they were either too little or too big. When Osiris finally stepped in – his proportions matched the chest perfectly.

This is when Set and his followers made their move! Once the King laid down the chest, they slammed it shut and soldered it with lead, trapping the king inside forever. The chest became his coffin and Set immediately bid his followers to get rid of the chest, throwing it into the Nile where it crashed across the waves, never to be found.

As can be expected, Isis was greatly shocked and saddened by what happened. Wearing her mourning robes, she made a vow to find the body of her husband and made this binding by cutting off a bow of her hair. She searched the lands, questioning every person she encountered but not receiving a positive response from any of them. Finally, she found out that the chest was washed off the Nile and entered the sea. Following the clues, Isis finally found her husband's coffin in Byblos, encased inside a tree. She took him back to Egypt in great secret, fearing that Set would do something worse to her husband's body. Nephthys was her confidante and while Isis gathered herbs to bring Osiris back to life with her magic, it was Nephthys' task to make sure that Set didn't find out about the body of the dead king.

Unfortunately, Set began to suspect the plot and despite Nephthys denying any knowledge, Set still managed to find the whereabouts of the coffin. He opened the chest and tore the dead body of Osiris apart, scattering the remains one by one into fourteen parts, although other stories claim that there were 42 parts in all. Regardless of the number, Set was happy with the way things turned out and went back to his kingdom.

When Isis returned, she was devastated to find that the body of Osiris was again missing with his parts scattered all over the world. Not giving up however, she searched every corner of the land – this time accompanied by Nephthys. Although it took a long time, Isis and Nephthys managed to find all but one of the body parts – Osiris's phallus (penis) was missing because it was swallowed by a fish. In an effort to protect each body part, Isis buried them on the spot where they were found, erecting a temple to mark the grave. According to stories, the 42 temples now mark the 42 provinces of Egypt.

When all the parts were gathered together, Isis sewed up her husband together and brought him to life. She made a replacement part for his missing phallus and they mated, resulting in the birth of Horus. Unfortunately, the fact that Osiris was no longer complete meant that he could no longer take the throne from Set. Instead, the once mighty king descended to the underworld where he is forever called the ruler of the land of the dead.

Fight of Set and Horus

Horus the Avenger was tasked at an early age to kill Set and avenge the death of his father. According to stories, his mother Isis made sure that Horus was hidden from Set as a young boy, fearing that he would be able to defeat the child before he grew to become a man. She hid him inside a lotus flower and bade him to be patient, promising to come back when the time was right.

Finally, the rest of the gods made inquiries, wanting to find out who would now be the ruler of the land with Osiris residing in the underworld. Although Horus was the rightful heir, Set argued that the child was too young and could therefore not rule Egypt properly. The gods were divided with the decision, Ra being on the side of Set while Hathor, Neith and the rest of the gods was in favor of Horus as the rightful king.

Ra being as powerful as he was, a final judgment was not achieved. Set, wanting to end it once and for all challenged Horus to a battle, confident that he would win against the man-child. The challenges were somewhat trivial and numerous, including who could hold their breath longer or who could magically turn themselves into an animal.

This is how the symbolic great eye of Horus came to be. During one of the battles, Set plucked out the left eye of Horus and Thoth came to his rescue, restoring his vision with the Light of the Moon. Next, Set again sent darkness on his right eye and this time, it was Hathor who came to his rescue. The goddess poured milk in his injured eye and claimed that this was the Light of the Sun.

In the stories, it was said that the contest between Set and Horus took 80 years to end. It concluded when finally, Set issued a last challenge to Horus, inviting the younger god outside for battle. Finally, Horus came back inside with Set bound in chains, dragging along behind him. Horus slew Set in front of the gods and thus, the great king Osiris was avenged and Horus claimed the throne as his.

Isis and the Scorpions

This story happened during the search of Isis for the body of Osiris. To protect the goddess, she had seven scorpions with her – three of which made sure the path ahead lay safe, two with Isis, and two more making sure that they were not followed. During this time, Isis greatly feared that Set would find them.

Isis was led to the Nile Delta by her search, aiming for the home of a wealthy noblewoman. However, when the woman saw the scorpions walking ahead, she was instantly terrified and shut the door on the goddess. One of the scorpions was not happy at this rudeness, sneaked inside and stung the child of the noblewoman – causing him to be on the brink of death.

The mother wailed in anguish and Isis – moved by the heartbreaking cry of a fellow mother – decided to help her. Using her magic, the goddess brought the child back to good health by whispering the name of each scorpion, therefore making their venom powerless against the child. This brought back the child to life and the wealthy woman thanked the goddess profusely, offering some of her wealth instead to the peasant girl who gave refuge to Isis during her time of need.

Chapter 4: Sphinx, Pharaohs, and Pyramids

Pharaohs

A good reason why pharaohs were so revered is because it is believed that they are the living link to the gods and goddesses. Bound by religion, the King is supposed to hold peace, harmony, and justice above all else. Seeing the world as surrounded by chaos, and pleasing their gods' through worship and offering, can help restore balance and essentially make their lives more peaceful and plenty.

Due to the fact that they are 'links to the gods' and essentially, much like gods themselves – it isn't surprising that the death of pharaohs are awarded much ceremony. More often than not, pharaohs are heavily invested into the idea of building their own pyramid and stacking it with gold and precious jewels to be brought to the afterlife.

Protecting the pharaoh before and after life were more than just duties – they were ways to prevent cosmic disturbance. It is believed that the current pharaoh is a representation of Horus and the dead father is Osiris. Together, the two would cause the sun to rise and set – and any disturbance could mean the sun not coming back up.

Pyramids

As you've read in the myth, pyramids are of great importance in Egypt because this was the first thing that emerged out of the sea of chaos. It is believed that the god Ra made the first pyramid, creating it to resemble the rays of the sun. Today, the pyramids are meant to protect the tombs of the kings and queens of Egypt, often loaded with gold and various items they have used in their lifetime. Since they were created for protection purposes, these pyramids have complicated layouts with the pharaoh protected in a heavy sarcophagus. The pyramids we see today are mere shadows of what they really looked like when they were created.

Mummification

Mummification has always fascinated people beyond Egypt and for a very good reason – the preservation of their bodies is incredibly well-made. Mummification serves one single need – to allow the spirit to still recognize his body in the afterlife.

Sphinx

The sphinx is often associated with Egypt – but did you know that Greece had its own sphinx? Typically, the creature is shown to have the body of a lion and the head of a woman. Unfortunately, the original purpose of the great Sphinx is unknown, although it's always been told that in stories that the Sphinx guarded a temple and would only allow entrance to anyone who provided the correct answer to a riddle. Today, the Sphinx is still a source of controversy with some people noting that the Great Sphinx of Giza is actually the head of a male and that its erection was a sign of power, validating the right of the pharaoh who had it made, to rule Egypt.

Conclusion

Thank you again for downloading this book!

I hope this book was able to help you learn more about Ancient Egyptian mythology!

Finally, if you enjoyed this book, please take the time to share your thoughts and post a review on Amazon. It'd be greatly appreciated!

Thank you and good luck!

www.ingramcontent.com/pod-product-compliance
Lightning Source LLC
Chambersburg PA
CBHW070739080526
44654CB00075B/1369